1,000
SIGNS
OF LIFE

1,000 SIGNS OF LIFE

Basic ASL for Everyday Conversation

BY THE EDITORS OF GALLAUDET UNIVERSITY PRESS

Gallaudet University Press
Washington, D.C.

Gallaudet University Press
Washington, DC 20002

http://gupress.gallaudet.edu

Library of Congress Cataloging in Publication Data

1,000 signs of life : basic ASL for everyday conversation / by the editors
of Gallaudet University Press.
     p. cm.
  ISBN 1-56368-272-9 (alk. paper)
  1. American Sign Language--Vocabulary. I. Title: 1000 signs of life. II. Title: One thousand signs of
life. III. Title: Basic ASL for everyday conversation. IV. Gallaudet University Press.
  HV2474.A12 2004
  419'.7--dc22

                                                                                          2004043294

The illustrations in this book are by Cherie Beaumont, Elissa Dawson, Gene Fontaine, Andrea
Grant, Christie Gymziak, Lois Lenderman, Mark Madigan, Julie O'Wril, Andrea Shine, Jan
Skrobisz, and William Woodson.

We also thank Meredyth Mustafa, Lance Hidy, Patrick McCarthy, and Claire Spellman for their
help with this book.

Cover photos by Sara R. Stallard

 ∞ The paper used in this publication meets the minimum requirements of American National Standard
for Information Sciences—Permanence of Paper for Printed Library Materials, ANSI Z39.48–1984

Contents

Introduction

1,000 Signs of Life offers new signers essential vocabulary for conversing in American Sign Language (ASL). It is a great way to start learning ASL on your own; it's also a perfect supplement for beginning sign language classes because it allows students to build their signing vocabularies while learning the structure of ASL. *1,000 Signs of Life* is arranged into seventeen different topic areas, with the signs organized in English alphabetical order. This format allows you to easily find a sign within a specific category. The word listed first is the one most commonly associated with the sign, but other synonyms are also included.

In addition to the signs, the book includes the American Manual Alphabet, the manual numbers, and an index of all the English words that correspond to the signs in the book. You will notice that some English words are listed several times, but with different page numbers. This is because an English word can have more than one meaning. For example, you can *run* a race, *run* the dishwasher, or *run* a company. In each case, the meaning of *run* is different, and, therefore, a different sign is used for each meaning.

What Is American Sign Language?

American Sign Language is a visual/gestural language used by many Deaf people in North America. ASL developed naturally over time, and it has all of the same features as other languages. It has specific rules for combining signs into sentences, such as beginning a sentence with a time sign and signing the subject before the verb. You will find other hints throughout the book to help you build sentences. All signed languages are unique and distinct languages that do not depend on speech or sound. They are not based on any spoken language, but like spoken languages, signed languages differ from country to country. ASL has its own lexicon (vocabulary), which includes idioms, slang, stylistic differences, and regional variations. We have included some examples of variation in this book.

Some ASL signs are formed with one hand, while others are formed with two hands. Signers use their naturally dominant hand to make one-hand signs. Some signs are made with two hands, but only the dominant hand moves. The illustrations in this dictionary show models with a right-hand dominance. If you are left-handed, simply mirror the sign illustrations.

Introduction

Sign Illustrations

Each sign entry includes one or more English words. These English words correspond to the conceptual meaning of the sign. Most of the illustrations include arrows that show how the hands move. A double-headed arrow (←→) means that the movement goes back and forth. A bent arrow or double arrows (Ꝺ, ⇉) are used when the movement is repeated. Curved arrows (↶) mean that the hands move in a circular motion instead of a straight line. Many signs move from an initial position to a final position. In this book, the first position is usually represented by light lines and the final position by darker lines. When signs have two distinct parts, as in TEACHER* (TEACH + person) or BELIEVE (THINK + AGREE), the parts are sometimes shown in one illustration and sometimes in side-by-side illustrations (see pages 53 and 140).

Signs Have Parts

Every sign is made up of five basic components or *parameters*. These parameters are *handshape, palm orientation, location, movement,* and *nonmanual signals*. If any of the five parameters change, the meaning of the sign also changes.

Handshape. The handshape is the most obvious part of a sign. The most frequently used handshapes are the letters of the American Manual Alphabet and the manual numbers (see figures 1 and 2), but there also are variations on some of these handshapes (for example, the Bent B used for REMIND on p. 193, and the Flat O used for EAT on p. 66), or combinations such as L and I (for AIRPLANE on p. 162), and 1 and I (for CAMPING on p. 162).

Palm Orientation. Orientation refers to the direction that the palm faces (up, down, left, or right). This is a useful way of describing the starting position of a sign. Once the palm is described, the placement of the fingers and back of the hand is obvious.

Location. Signs are formed on or near only certain areas of the body. Approximately 75 percent of all signs are formed between the head and the chest, where they can be seen more easily. The location of a sign frequently contributes to its meaning. For example, many signs that represent feelings are made near the heart, whereas signs related to thought processes are made near the head.

Movement. Meaning also can be expressed through movement. The direction in which a sign moves may indicate who is giving or receiving the

---

* ASL signs are written in small capital letters to represent their English meaning.

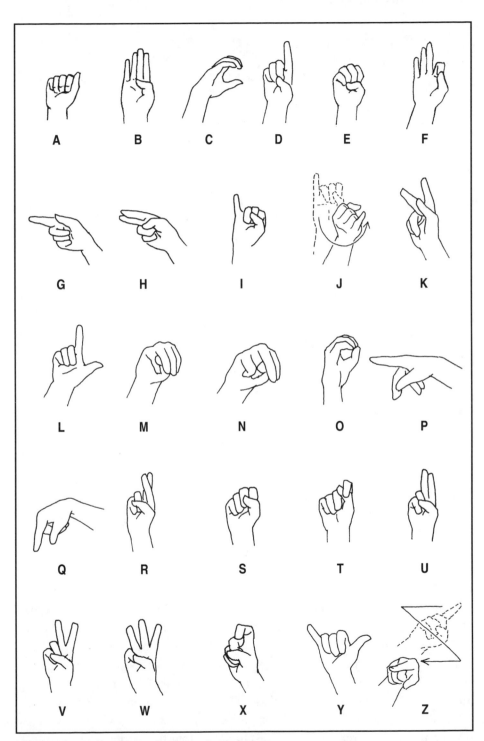

Figure 1. The American Manual Alphabet

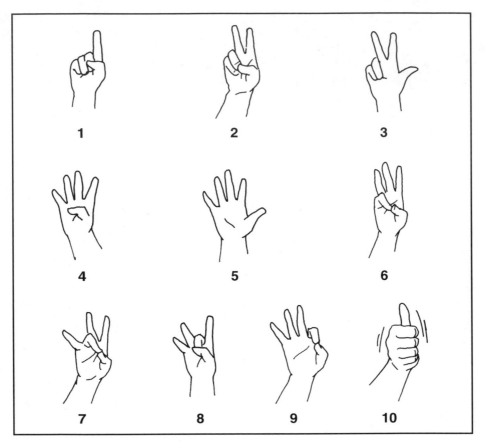

Figure 2. The Manual Numbers

action of a verb. For example, if the sign HELP moves out from the signer, that means the signer is offering help to someone. If the sign moves in toward the signer, it means someone is helping the signer.

The repetition of the movement may indicate several things—the frequency of an action, the difference between singular and plural, or the distinction between a noun and a verb. The size of the movement can show volume or size, and the speed of the repetition combined with the appropriate facial expressions may convey whether the action was completed quickly or slowly. Generally, the signs in this book show basic movements.

Nonmanual Signals. Being a good signer involves more than just executing signs correctly. In spoken languages, the tone of the speaker's voice adds additional meaning to the message. In signed languages, additional information is carried through the signer's body and facial expressions. This nonmanual parameter occurs at the same time that the sign is produced to contribute to its meaning. The signed message is quite different if you shake your head no or nod your head yes while signing HUNGRY.

Fingerspelling

While ASL is not a code for English, it does have a way to include English words. This is done by spelling words with one hand. The American Manual Alphabet has a handshape to represent each letter of the English alphabet (see page 3), and signers use this alphabet to spell out English words. This is called *fingerspelling*. Signers fingerspell when a particular concept, like a proper name, a brand name, or a relatively new idea or product does not have a sign. Technical terms are fingerspelled only if no sign currently exists and/or it is important to know the exact English term.

It's important to hold your hand steady when you fingerspell. Keep it at mid-chest level, take your time, and try not to say the names of the individual letters as you sign them. Practice in front of a mirror to see both the expressive and receptive perspectives at the same time. Most people find it easier to fingerspell than to read someone else's fingerspelling. When you read someone's fingerspelling, it helps to remember that this is similar to reading words on a page. Whether you realize it or not, you do not read letter by letter, you see whole words and the configuration of words or phrases. In addition, you use context. The principles of learning how to read apply to reading fingerspelling as well. Don't look for individual letters when someone is fingerspelling, look for clues, such as the length of a word, its position in the sentence, the configuration of the word, easily recognized letters and letter combinations (like *–ing*, and *–tion*), and sentence context to help you make an educated guess.

Practice, Practice, Practice

Learning ASL is similar to learning a spoken language—you have to use the language a lot before you can become fluent. *1,000 Signs of Life* will give you a good start on your signing vocabulary. Use it to learn new signs and then refer to it to refresh your memory. Of course, the best way to learn ASL is to converse with a deaf person, but when you can't, review the signs in *1,000 Signs of Life* to prepare for your next encounter.

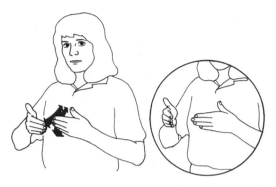

Anyhow, anyway, doesn't matter, even though, in spite of, nevertheless, no matter, regardless

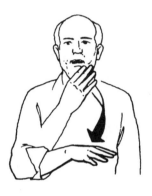

Bad, naughty, poor

Beautiful, gorgeous

Best

Better

Adjectives/Adverbs

Big, large

Bright, clear, light

Busy

Careless, reckless

Cheap, inexpensive

Clean, nice, pure, tidy

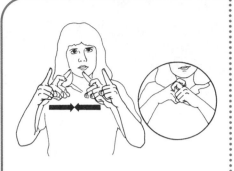

Complex, complicated

Confused

Crazy, absurd

Crazy-for

Cute

Dangerous

Adjectives/Adverbs

Different

Difficult, hard, problem, rough, tough

Dirty

Dizzy

Dry, arid

Easy, simple

Even, fair, tie

Far, distant

Fast, immediate, rapid, speedy, swift

Fun, leisure, recreation

Funny, amusing, humorous

Good, benevolent

Adjectives/Adverbs

Hard (substance)

Hot

Inferior

Interesting

Little (height), short, small

Little (size), small, tiny

Long, length

Lucky, fortunate

Maybe, might, perhaps

Mischievous, naughty

Necessary

New, fresh

Adjectives/Adverbs

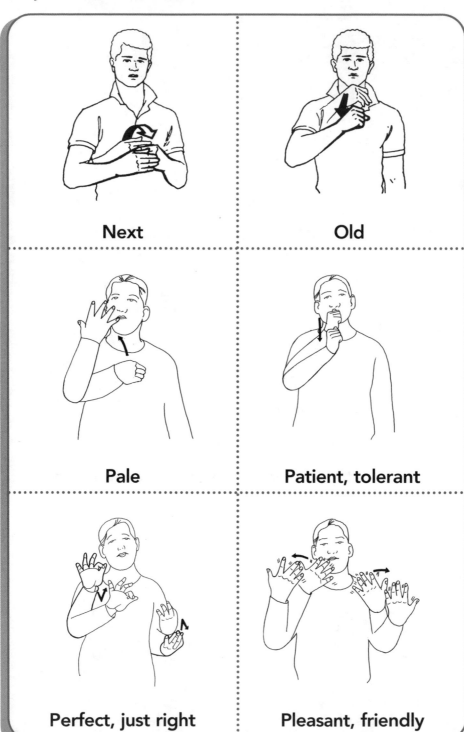

Next

Old

Pale

Patient, tolerant

Perfect, just right

Pleasant, friendly

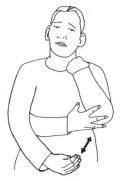

Poor, destitute, impoverished

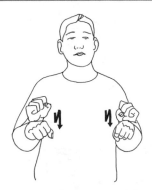

Possible, possibly, probably

Pretty, attractive, lovely

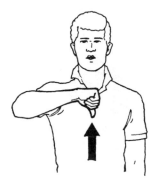

Proud, arrogant, pride

Quick, fast, immediately, quickly

Quiet, peaceful, silent, still

Adjectives/Adverbs

Ready

Real, genuine, sure

Really, true

Relieved, relief

Rich, wealthy

Right, accurate, correct

Rough, coarse, crude, draft

Safe, free, redeem, salvation, secure

Same, also, like, too

Same, alike, similar

Serious

Silly, absurd, ridiculous

Look at Me!

Deaf people have a number of strategies for getting one another's attention—and some of them are quite shocking to hearing people who encounter them for the first time. One of the first surprises is that being deaf doesn't necessarily mean sound is irrelevant. On the contrary, it most certainly is, especially when it's loud and vibrant. In deaf-oriented environments, low-pitched hooting or shouting is common—especially among deaf people who wear hearing aids.

Tables and other surfaces such as wooden floors are great conductors. They carry the vibrations created by sound waves, and they make great mediums for pounding and stomping to get someone's attention. In fact, some deaf families have designed homes with wooden floors for just this purpose. Another strategy is to install light flashers around the house, so family members can call to each other from other rooms. Gallaudet University designed their classrooms with light switches by the blackboards for this reason, as well. Table-pounding also occurs in classes, cafeterias, and other places, even in restaurants (much to the chagrin of certain people).

Waving is the most immediate means of getting attention in person. But, there are a few considerations that must be heeded:

1. Never wave right in someone's face—it's too mentally jarring to be acceptable, even among deaf-blind people.
2. Don't wave for a prolonged duration—a person who doesn't respond right away is busy at the moment.
3. If someone is waving for your attention and you can't attend right away, indicate "wait" or "one moment" by holding up your index finger. The person waving for you will know you have acknowledged his or her presence and thus will await his or her turn.

The "wait" signal is also used in the middle of a conversation, when one person notices something happening in the background and wants to take a moment to observe the scene. It's not a sign of impoliteness but rather a significant need on deaf people's part to be aware of the environment around them.

Similar, common, in common

Simple

Single, unmarried

Slippery

Slow, slowly

Adjectives/Adverbs

Soft

Solid

Standard, uniform

Strict, rigid

Tall (object)

Tall (person)

That

Thin

This

Tired, exhausted, fatigued, weary, worn out

Tough, very difficult

Ugly

Adjectives / Adverbs

Ugly

Wet, damp, moist, moisture

Whew!

Wonderful, marvelous, terrific

Wrong, mistake, mistaken

Bird, chicken, hen

Cat

Cow

Dinosaur

Dog

Eagle

Animals

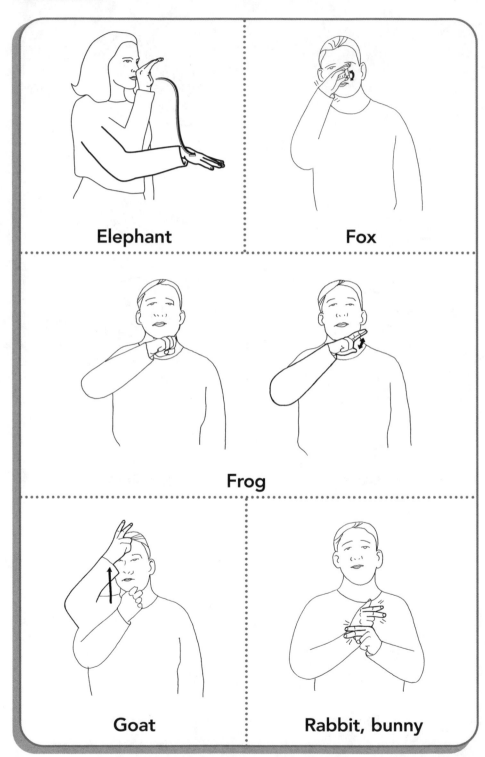

Elephant

Fox

Frog

Goat

Rabbit, bunny

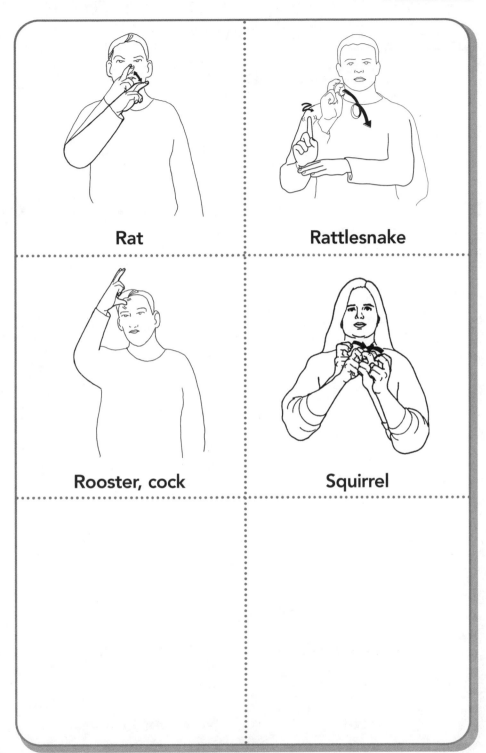

Rat

Rattlesnake

Rooster, cock

Squirrel

Incorporating Gender

In some ways, ASL is more closely related to languages other than English in its structure. One example is in the way those languages incorporate the gender of the subject or object into the base form of a word. For example, while English uses the word *cousin* to indicate all cousins, both male and female, French has two words—*cousin* for male cousins and *cousine* for female cousins. Similarly, ASL distinguishes between male and female nouns by location. Many of the signs for females are located or originate on the lower part of the face. These include GIRL, WOMAN, MOTHER, GRANDMOTHER, DAUGHTER, AUNT, NIECE, and GIRL-COUSIN. Signs for males are located or originate near the forehead, and these include BOY, MAN, FATHER, GRANDFATHER, SON, UNCLE, NEPHEW, and BOY-COUSIN.

Female cousin

Male cousin

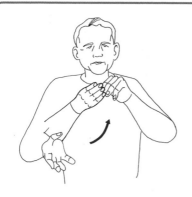

Add, addition

America

And

Answer, reply, response

Article

Attention, focus, pay attention

Classroom Vocabulary

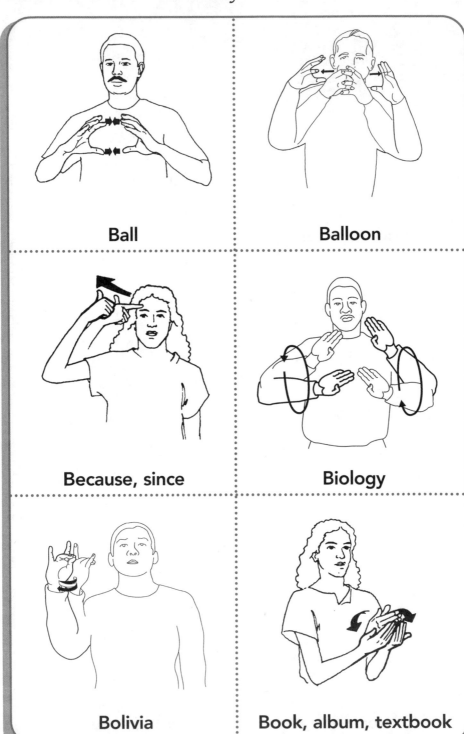

Ball

Balloon

Because, since

Biology

Bolivia

Book, album, textbook

Break, intermission

But

Canada

Center, middle, seat

Center, central

Chair, seat

Classroom Vocabulary

Check (v), inspect

Chemistry

Choice

Class

College

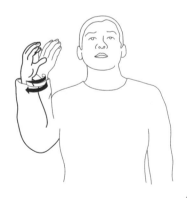

Colombia

Communication

Communist

Congratulations

Constitution

Correct, accurate, right

Count

Classroom Vocabulary

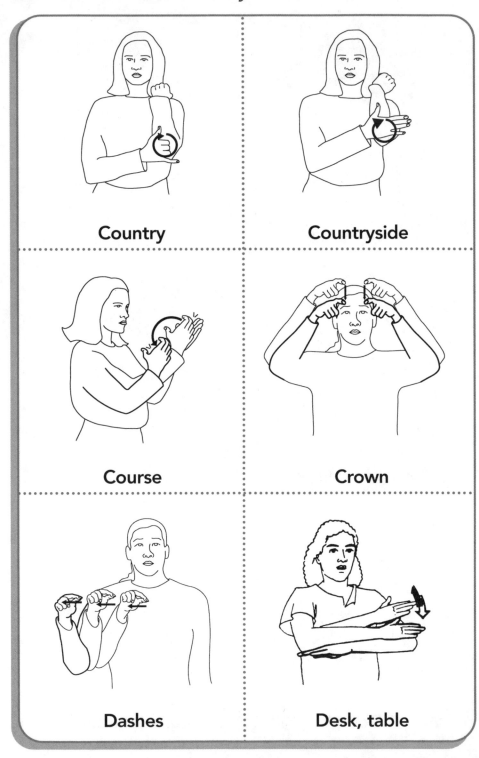

Country

Countryside

Course

Crown

Dashes

Desk, table

Dictionary

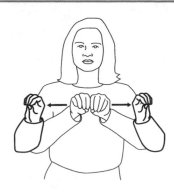

Diploma, degree

Divide, split

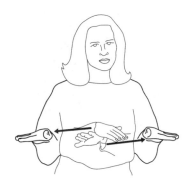

Don't

Door

Drops (of liquid)

Classroom Vocabulary

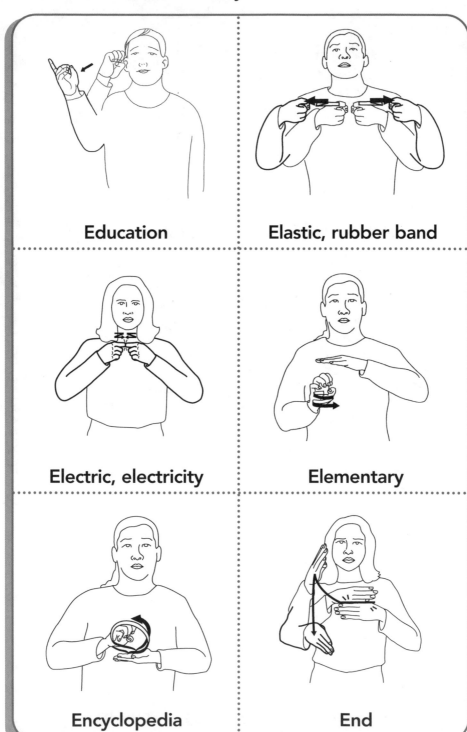

Education

Elastic, rubber band

Electric, electricity

Elementary

Encyclopedia

End

England, English

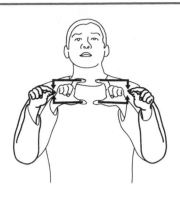

Envelope

Erase

Erase

Exchange, instead, replace, substitute

Excuse me

Classroom Vocabulary

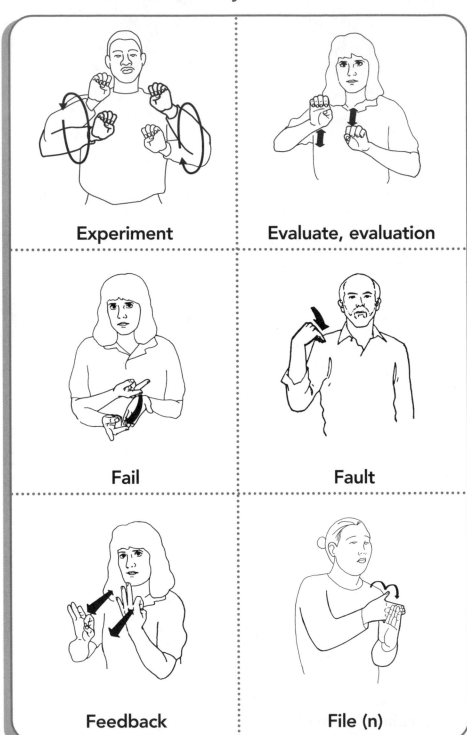

Experiment

Evaluate, evaluation

Fail

Fault

Feedback

File (n)

Fingerspell

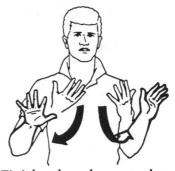

Finish, already, complete, did, done, enough, have, over, stop it, through

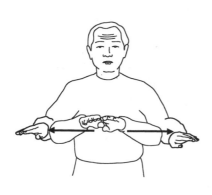

Floor, ground

Form (paper)

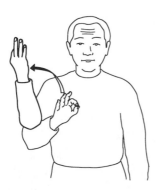

France (French)

Function

English as a Friend of ASL

The sign translated as *group* shares the same movement, location, and orientation as the signs that translate into the English words *association, class, family,* and *organization*. These words have a similar conceptual meaning, thus they are produced with the handshape of the initial letter of the corresponding English word. Another group of words that share similar meaning and sign parameters except for handshape are *law, principle,* and *rule*.

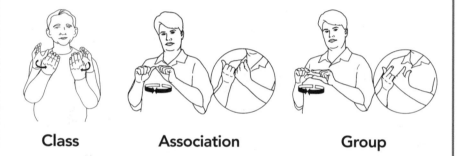

Class   **Association**   **Group**

It may seem odd that proponents of ASL would use obvious English markers when signing, but this is comparable to how English itself borrows words from other languages—in fact, more than half of the current English lexicon is of foreign origin. This is important to remember, especially when we come across an English word that cannot be translated into sign. When this happens, the word must be fingerspelled in the American manual alphabet.

This does not, in any way, diminish the use of ASL; in fact, it enhances our use of ASL, making deaf people and new hearing signers bilingual or multilingual. ASL signs alone represent concepts, not English words, but the two are found together in the vernacular of many signers. This is commonly called contact signing, but in essence it is still ASL, just with plenty of English flavor, as evident in the mouthing of English words and in the frequent use of fingerspelled words. Calling this ASL with an English dialect or accent might be more appropriate.

Germany

Help, aid, assist

Holland

Important, crucial, key, main, significant, valuable, value, worth, worthwhile

Improve

Information, inform, let know, notify

Classroom Vocabulary

Introduce, present

Israel

Keep

Kind, type

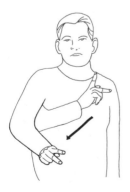

King

Know, aware, conscious, familiar, knowledge

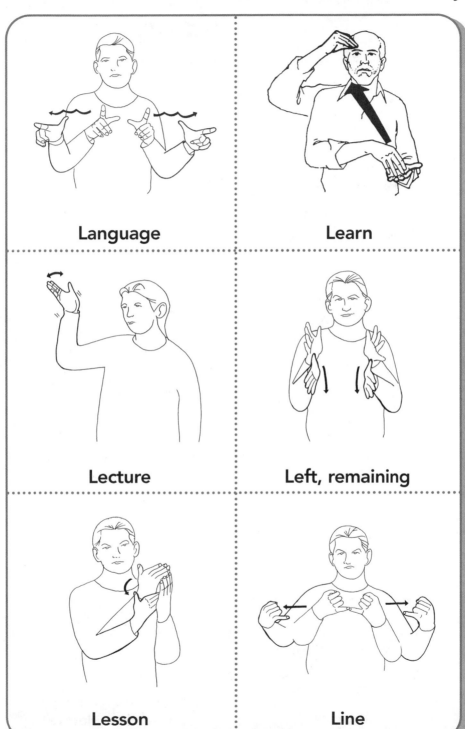

Language

Learn

Lecture

Left, remaining

Lesson

Line

Classroom Vocabulary

Magazine, brochure, catalog, journal, pamphlet

Major, area, main, specialty

Match

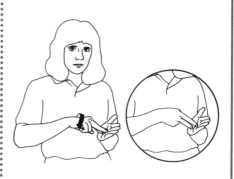

Meaning, intend, mean, purpose

Measure

Message

Microphone

Mistake, error

Name, call, mention

Nation, native

Newspaper, press, printing, publish

No

Classroom Vocabulary

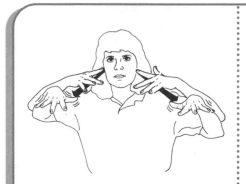

Noise, noisy

Not, don't

Number

Ocean

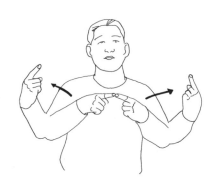

Opposite, contrary, contrast

Oral

Paper

Parallel

Patient, bear, put up with, stand, tolerant, tolerate

Pencil

Peru

Piano

Classroom Vocabulary

Picture, photograph

Plant, spring

Please

ASL poetry

Poster, chart, notice

Poster, form

Present, gift

Pressure

Principal

Privilege

Problem, problematic, difficulty, troublesome

Program

Classroom Vocabulary

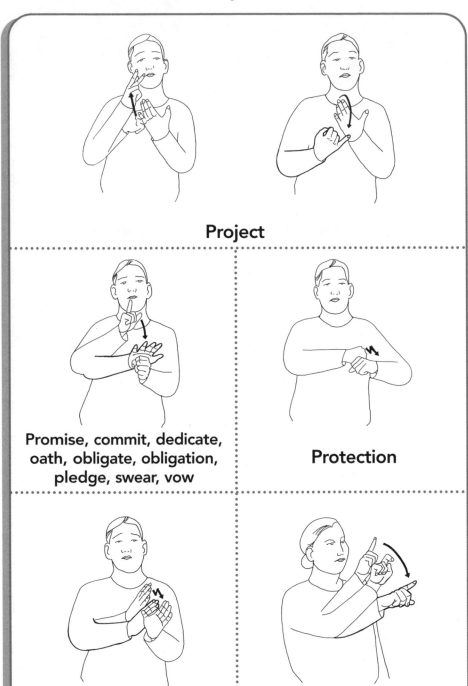

Project

Promise, commit, dedicate, oath, obligate, obligation, pledge, swear, vow

Protection

Psychology

Question

Reading

Record (n)

Require, demand, insist

Research

Residential school, institute, institution, school for the deaf

Respect

Classroom Vocabulary

Responsibility, in charge, responsible

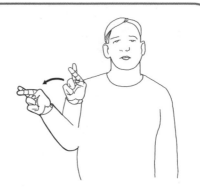

Restroom

Rock

Room

Roots

Rule, regulation

Schedule, chart

School, academic,
academy

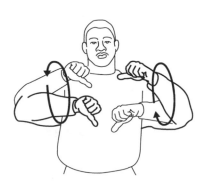

science

Secret, confidential,
personal, private

Sentence

Serious discussion

Classroom Vocabulary

Share

Sit, sit down

Skill, expert, talent

Spelling

Steam

Stop, cease

Story

Student

Teach, educate, instruct

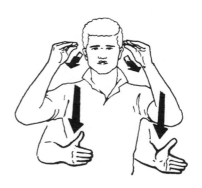

Teacher

Thank you

Thing

Classroom Vocabulary

Typewriter

Wait

Weigh, weight

Word

**Xerography,
photocopy, scan**

Yes

Blouse

Clothes

Coat

Dress (v)

Leather

Pants

Clothes

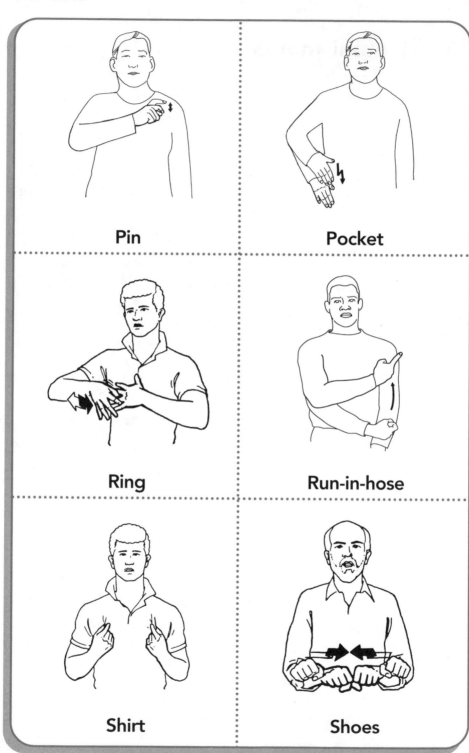

Pin

Pocket

Ring

Run-in-hose

Shirt

Shoes

Visual Impairments

Deaf people who have vision impairments have different interpreting needs in order to participate in meetings, classes, and other events. Many require close-up interpreting, meaning the interpreter must sit very close to the deaf person. Deaf people who are also blind need tactile interpreting—they place one or both hands on the interpreter's hands. ASL is a tactile as well as visual language, and deaf-blind people are fully capable of carrying on a conversation through touching your hands. Some are so skilled they need only touch the area between your thumb and forefinger, instead of covering your entire hand—muscle contractions differ enough to indicate which fingers are being flexed and how the hand is moving.

No matter which type of interpreting is used, the physical space may have to be rearranged to accommodate the interpreter. Sometimes this means moving furniture or asking for front-row privileges. At the same time, the visual needs of other deaf people must be kept in mind.

Aside from the considerations mentioned above, it's important to treat deaf people with visual impairments just as you would any other deaf person. Call for their attention by tapping them on the shoulder. Don't wave your hand directly in front of someone's face—just get into their line of vision and signal for their attention as you would for anybody else. If the person is deaf-blind, you may put your hand on his shoulder to indicate your presence and wait for him to free his hands for conversing with you, or place your hand(s) under his—don't grab onto his hand!

Usher syndrome is one of the leading causes of deaf-blindness. It is a hereditary disease that usually begins with deafness at birth. While Usher syndrome is rare, there are deaf families where it is a fact of life, appearing generation after generation. As children with Usher's grow older, their visual fields begin to narrow. The eventual result can be total or near total blindness. People with Usher's usually see well enough in youth to become fluent in sign language. You cannot really tell that a person has Usher's until she starts using a white cane or other assistive devices. This can cause confusion for newcomers to Deaf culture because they will see this person signing like any other deaf person, but when they try to call for her attention, by waving from a distance or off on the side, they are ignored. The person with Usher syndrome isn't being rude—she simply may not see you.

Clothes

Shorts

Skirt

Sleeves

Socks

Wear

Wear

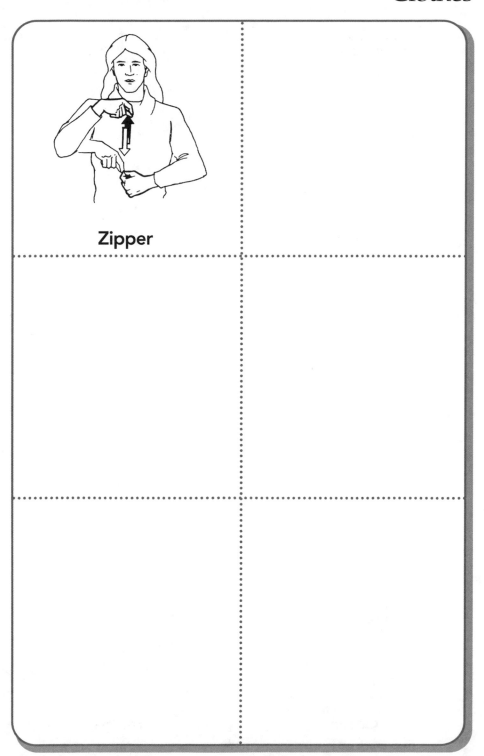

Zipper

Colors

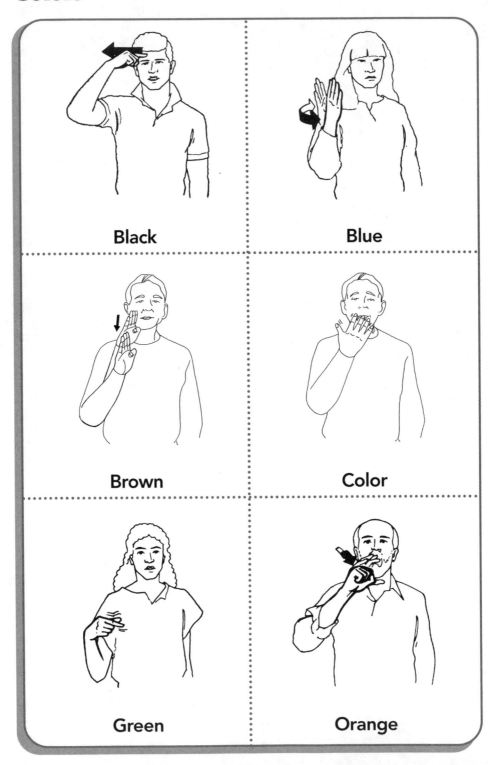

Black

Blue

Brown

Color

Green

Orange

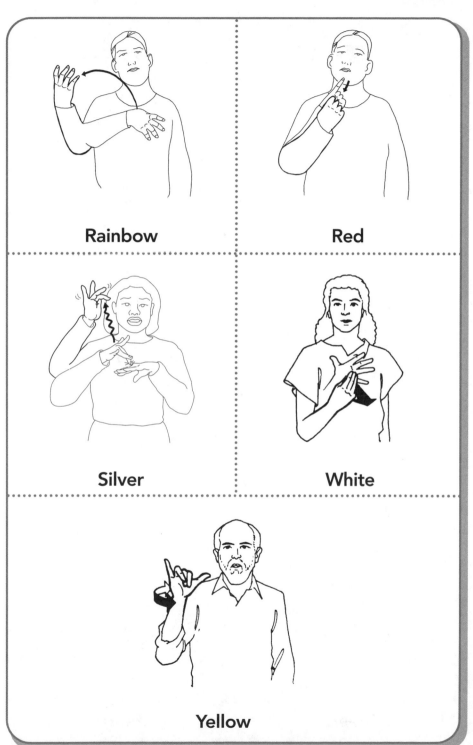

Rainbow

Red

Silver

White

Yellow

Food

Apple

Bacon

Bake

Banana

Beans

Beer

Bitter, sour

Bread

Breakfast

Butter

Cake

Candy

Food

Candy cane

Carrot

Cheese

Chicken

Coffee

Cook

Cookie

Cracker

Cup

Dinner

Food

Drink

Eat, food

Egg

Fork

Glass

Hungry

Ice cream

Jelly

Kitchen

Knife

Lunch

Meat, beef, flesh, steak

Food

Milk

Napkin

Peach

Pear

Pepper

Light and Space

Good lighting is very important for signers. You may have heard that the kitchen is the classic gathering place for Deaf people because the light usually is bright and the space is good for a small group of people to stand around and chat—while they raid the refrigerator, of course. In addition to the kitchen, porches and wide hallways are great places for conversation, and no doubt, these places contribute to the concept of DST (Deaf Standard Time) a quaint and often abused excuse for long, lingering good-byes.

Out in public spaces, the sidewalk usually takes the place of the porch after an event in a restaurant or a club. Try to observe how signers move around when they sign—out of the shadows, out of direct light, away from glare, etc. Bright light coming from behind the signer makes it hard for the listener to see the signer's face. During a conversation outside, signers will rotate their positions until the light falls on both of them from the side.

Signers in restaurants and coffee shops usually prefer well-lit tables. They avoid sitting next to the wall in order to have plenty of elbow room, and they try to keep the table free of tall vases, candlesticks, and condiment bottles. These items obstruct vision and are susceptible to being knocked over.

When and if you sign on stage or before an audience, remember to stand in the spotlight, even if you cannot see your listeners—just step out of the light momentarily to field questions and comments from your audience. Try to stand in one spot—walking around or shifting your feet can be very distracting. Wear solid colors that create a nice contrast to your skin color, in order to make your hands and face stand out. For example, fair skin looks clearer against navy, maroon, evergreen, or black; dark skin looks clearer against pastel hues. Try to avoid white—it can be too bright and overpowering.

In classes or discussion groups that mainly cater to signers, you will almost always see the seats arranged in a circular shape. This is especially true at Gallaudet University, the National Technical Institute for the Deaf, and deaf schools throughout the world. Instructors sometimes arrange desks in rows and columns when they present a lecture. This arrangement discourages side conversations, and it is also the most appropriate way to administer examinations.

Food

Pie

Pitcher

Plate

Popcorn

Salt

Slice

Soda, pop

Spicy

Spoon

Sprinkles

Steam

Food

Sugar

Sweet

Tea

Thirsty

Water

Wine

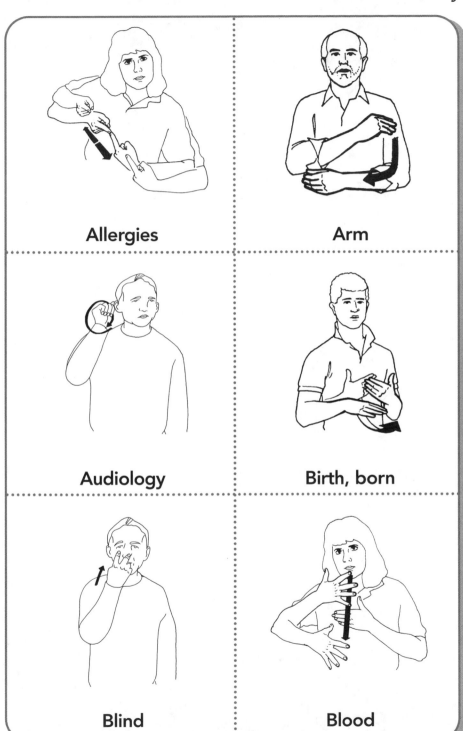

Allergies

Arm

Audiology

Birth, born

Blind

Blood

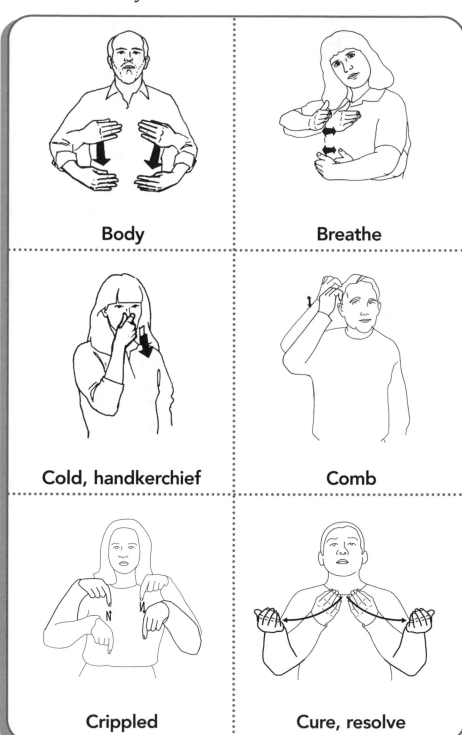

Body

Breathe

Cold, handkerchief

Comb

Crippled

Cure, resolve

Cut

Dead

Deaf

Deaf

Dentist

Doctor

Health/Body

Ear

Eye

Face

Fever

Glasses

Hair

Hands

Hard of hearing

Head

Hear, ear, hearing, sound

Hearing aid

Hearing person

Health/Body

Heart

Height

Hurt, ache

Life, live

Medicine, medication

Mouth

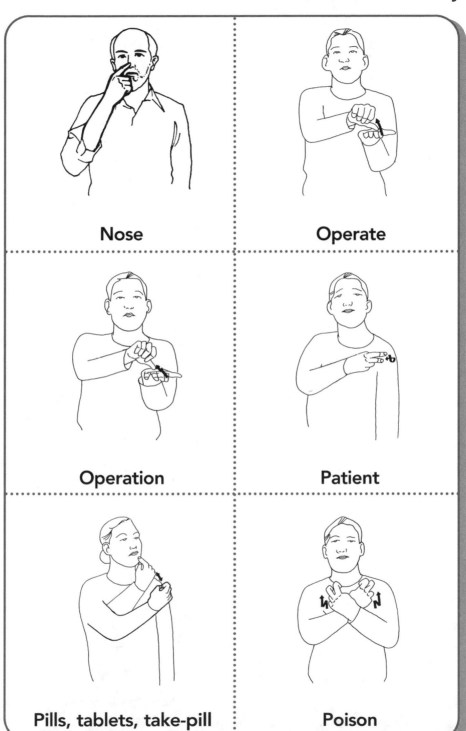

Nose

Operate

Operation

Patient

Pills, tablets, take-pill

Poison

Health/Body

Powder

Recover

Runny nose

See

Sex

Sick, disease, ill, illness, sickness

Skin

Sleep, asleep

Smell

Sneeze

An Alternative Language Choice

As more research on cognitive brain function and language is being done, the benefits of sign language continue to become more and more evident. ASL is now considered a viable language for people with disabilities other than deafness, such as developmental disabilities or delays, autism, brain damage, or loss of the voice. Teachers in special education as well as regular education classrooms are incorporating sign language into their daily communication. Teachers have found that signs help all children develop their reading, vocabulary, and spelling skills faster and more efficiently.

It is also now known that babies are capable of using their hands for communication well before they can speak. The result of early expressive language is less frustration and more communicative exchanges between infant and parents. Preschool and day care programs have begun to incorporate signs into their classrooms. Children as young as nine months have used signs to indicate when they want their bottle or want to eat. A growing number of hearing parents are realizing the advantages of early meaningful communication, and they are teaching their hearing babies to sign. Sign classes for parents and their babies are popping up around the country.

Speech, oral

Tongue

Voice

Young, youth

Holidays/Religion

Angel

Baptist

Bible

Catholic

Christian

Devil

Easter

God

Jew, Jewish

Holidays/Religion

Lord

Methodist

Mission

Nun

Pray

Preach

Signing Songs

One of the most popular performance applications for ASL is signed songs. Signing choirs can be found all over the country—from elementary schools to universities, from churches to gospel groups that travel the country. Every year the *Star Spangled Banner* is performed at countless events, including the Super Bowl.

Translating a song into ASL means taking certain liberties with standard English structure. ASL relies on the conceptual meaning of the lyrics, not how the lyrics are strung together. Words like *oh, the, by, to,* and forms of *to be* cannot be translated into ASL because signs do not exist for these words. While fingerspelling works well while conversing, it's awkward while "singing," so signers avoid fingerspelling in signed songs. Signers have to really think about the meaning of a song before translating it into ASL.

Try signing the following translation of the *Star Spangled Banner*. In this version, QUESTION is signed for the rhetorical phrase, "Oh say." Later in the song, the signs OH and HEY are signed as WHAT, where the hands are held out with palms up and the face not so much questioning as showing affirmation of the fact.

QUESTION, YOU EXPERT SEE
O say, can you see,
SUNRISE BRIGHT
by the dawn's early light,
THAT REAL PROUD WE HONOR
What so proudly we hailed
CONTINUE SUNSET FADE
at the twilight's last gleaming?
RED WHITE STRIPES STAR SPECKLE
Whose broad stripes and bright stars,
THROUGH BATTLE AWFUL
through the perilous fight,
STAND BRIDGE WE WATCHING
O'er the ramparts we watched,
WOW BRAVE FLAG-WAVING
were so gallantly streaming?

HEY, CANNON RED ROCKET
And the rockets' red glare,
EXPLODE EXPLODE IN AIR-SKY
the bombs bursting in air,
THROUGH ALL-NIGHT PROOF
Gave proof through the night
OUR FLAG STILL THERE!
That our flag was still there.
OH, QUESTION, OUR STAR SPECKLE
    FLAG STILL WAVE
O say, does that star-spangled banner
    yet wave
OVER LAND FREE
O'er the land of the free
HOME THEIR BRAVE?
And the home of the brave?

Holidays/Religion

Preacher

Presbyterian

Priest

Resurrection

Savior

Thanksgiving

Actor, actress

Address

Alarm

Appointment

Area

Around here, region, vicinity

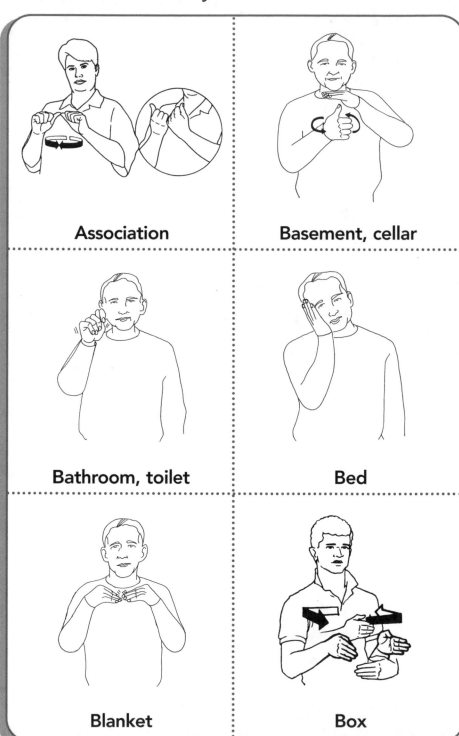

Association

Basement, cellar

Bathroom, toilet

Bed

Blanket

Box

Business

City, town, village

Court, judge (v), justice, trial

Courthouse

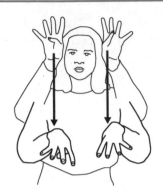

Curtains, drapes

Democrat

Department

Drawer

Elevator

Enemy, foe, opponent, rival

Fence

Fire

Flower, rose

Football

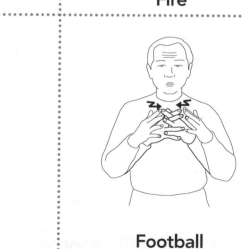

Home/Community

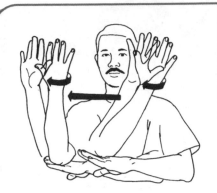

Forest, woods

Foundation

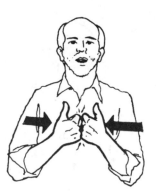

Game, match

Good-bye

Government

Grass

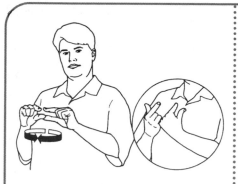

Group

Happen, coincidence, event, incident, occur, occurrence

Highway

Home

Hospital

House

Jail

Job

Job, work

Key

Law, legal

Letter, mail

Library

Machine, engine, factory, mechanical, mechanism, plant

Matchstick

Meeting, convention, session

Meter (utility)

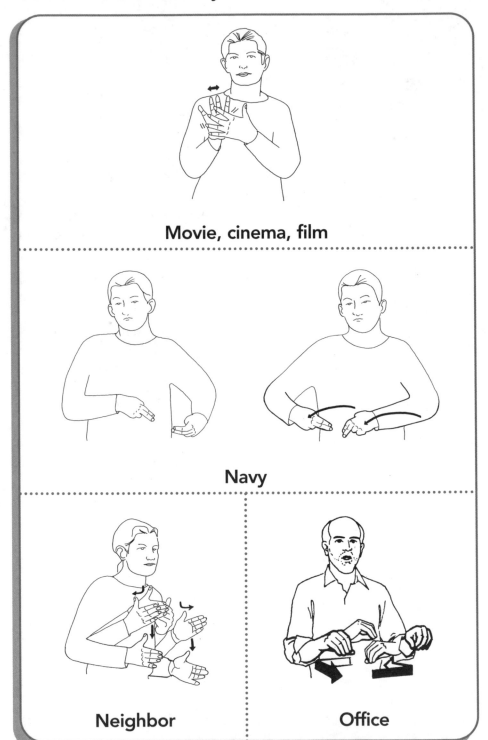

Movie, cinema, film

Navy

Neighbor

Office

Parade, procession

Party

Peace, calm, peaceful, serene

Pinball

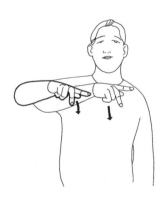

Ping pong

Police, cop, officer, sheriff

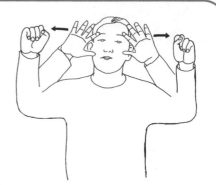

President, superintendent

Prison

Radio

Rent, monthly

Republican

Reservation

Restaurant

Right, entitled

Rollerblading

Rollerskating

Roof

Running water

Screwdriver

Secretary

Seesaw

Shelf, mantle

Society

Better Life Through Technology

Deaf people have benefited greatly from electronic devices designed to increase their access to the world at large. Their homes are equipped with gadgets that let them know when someone is at the door, when the phone is ringing, when the baby is crying, and when the smoke detector goes off. The greatest boon to communication came with the invention of the teletypewriter for the deaf (TTY), which allowed deaf people to use a telephone to contact each other. The late-20th century saw the emergence of relay services that further increased deaf people's access to the outside world. The relay allows a TTY user to place a call to a hearing person, or vice versa, using the relay operator as an intermediary.

The digital age has made possible a slew of communicative devices that benefit deaf people in incredible and far-reaching ways. Instant messaging, e-mail, and two-way pagers have become the norm for those in urban areas or with access to computers. Some people now use their TTY only on rare occasions.

English is not the only language that deaf people can utilize with today's technology. There is a growing demand for computer and electronic tools that facilitate communication in ASL. Video conferencing came onto the scene in the 1990s, enabling colleges, universities, and other professional programs to hold meetings or discussions across distances. Now that more people have signed up for high-speed internet services, webcams are becoming another tool in deaf people's communication arsenal. The rate of data transfer is fast enough to enable normal signing, in most cases. Relay services have added ASL-to-voice interpreting, allowing deaf and hearing people to converse via a webcam. The webcam also can be used to send video e-mails to friends, family, and colleagues—as well as for posting videos on the Internet.

With visual devices such as webcams and sophisticated camcorders, ASL is no longer limited to physical location, but can now be utilized as regularly as English. Once the realm of science fiction films and television programs, video phones are becoming a reality. And even though some people may worry that they have to shower and get dressed before they answer the phone, this technology will provide deaf people with yet more options for face-to-face communication.

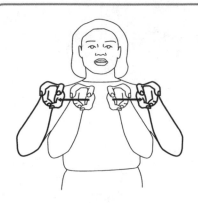

Sofa, couch

Store, shop, shopping

Street, avenue, road

Team

Telephone

Ticket

Television, TV

Tree

Vote, elect, election

Wall

Window

People

Adopt, assume, take up

Adult

Anyone

Baby

Bachelor

Birthday

Boy

Boyfriend

Brother

Brother

People

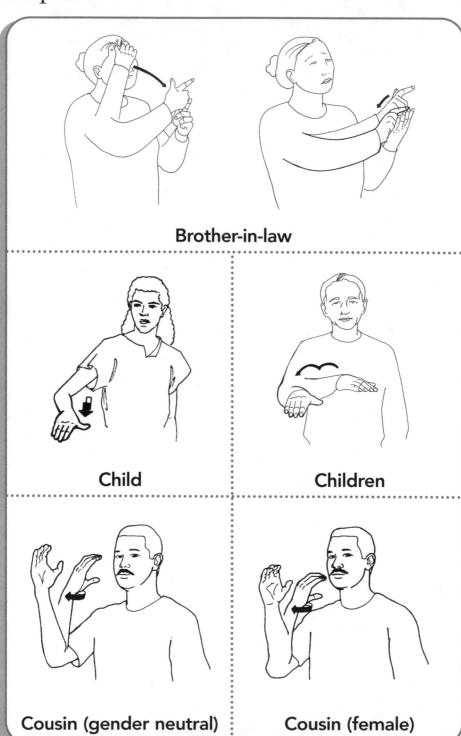

Brother-in-law

Child

Children

Cousin (gender neutral)

Cousin (female)

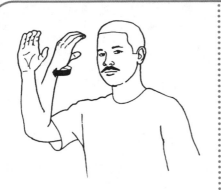

Cousin (male)

Daughter

Divorce

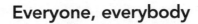

Everyone, everybody

People

Everyone, everybody (in a group)

Family

Father

Father-in-law

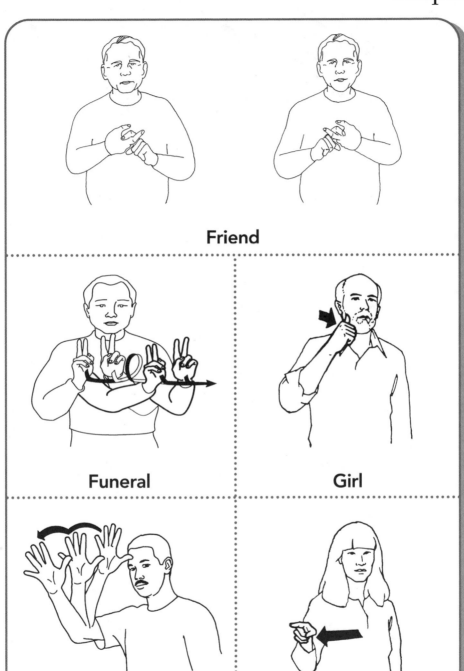

Friend

Funeral

Girl

Grandfather

He, her, him, it, she

People

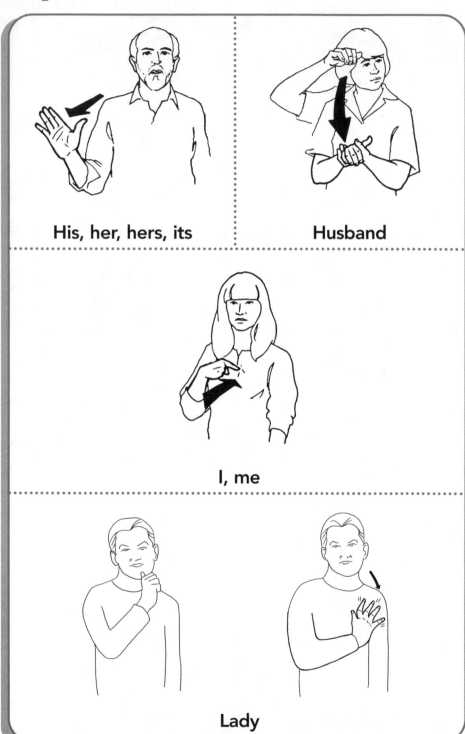

His, her, hers, its

Husband

I, me

Lady

Looks (appears)

Looks (appearance)

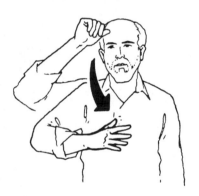

Man

Mother

My, mine

Our, ours

Compounds

One way to create new words in a spoken language is to combine existing words. This new combination, called a *compound*, creates a word that takes on a meaning independent of its component parts. Examples of compound words in English include *playground*, *greenhouse*, and *someone*. ASL allows for the creation of compound signs. These compounds are created when two individual signs are combined to create a third sign with an entirely different meaning. Some examples of compound signs are listed below.

GIRL + MARRY = WIFE

BOY + MARRY = HUSBAND

MOTHER + FATHER = PARENTS

GIRL + SAME = SISTER

BOY + SAME = BROTHER

THINK + MARRY = BELIEVE

THINK + SAME = AGREE

Parents

Agree

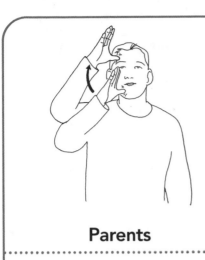

Parents

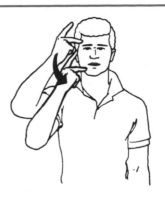

Parents

People

Person

Personality

Photographer

People

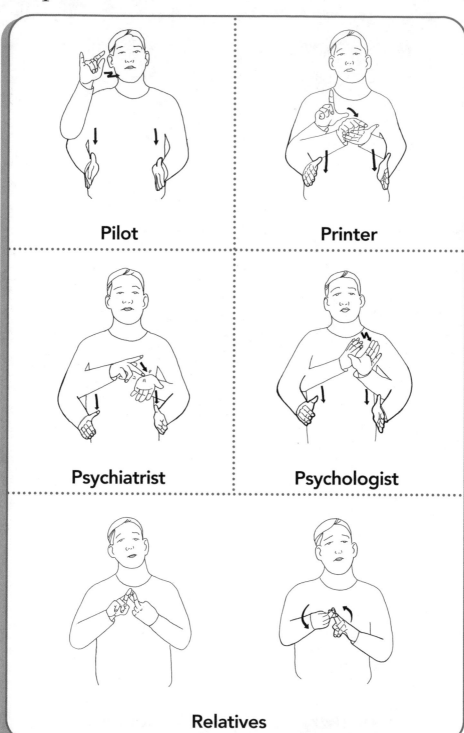

Pilot

Printer

Psychiatrist

Psychologist

Relatives

Reporter

Sister

Son

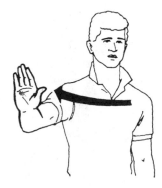

Their, theirs

They, them

We, us

People

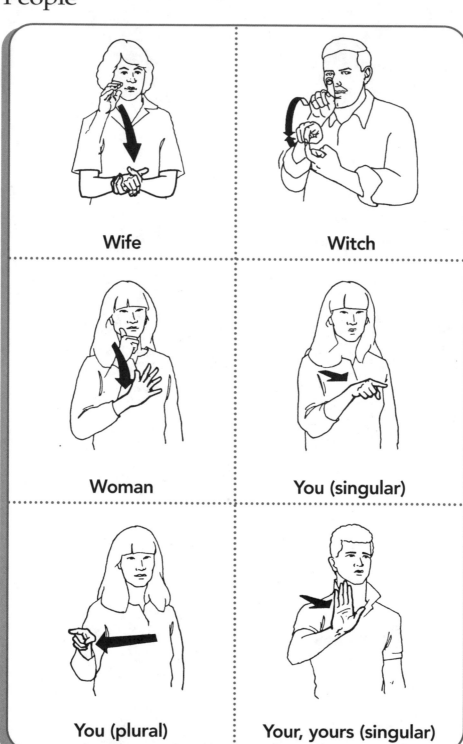

Wife

Witch

Woman

You (singular)

You (plural)

Your, yours (singular)

Your, yours (plural)

Prepositions/Locations

About, concerning

Above, over

Across, cross, over

Among, amid

Around, orbit, surround

Around, about, approximately

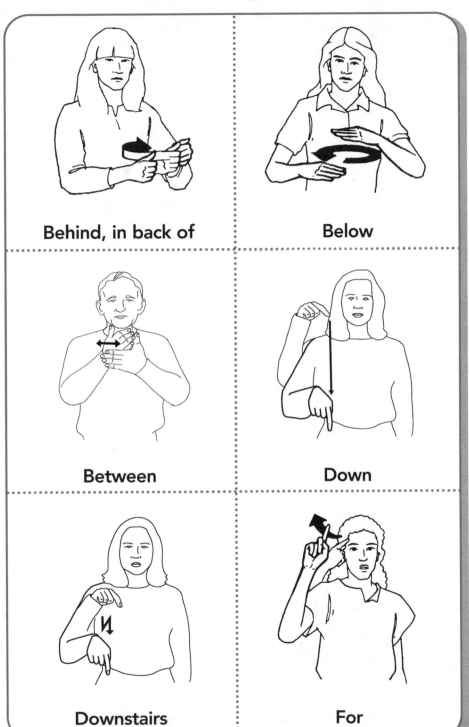

Behind, in back of

Below

Between

Down

Downstairs

For

Prepositions/Locations

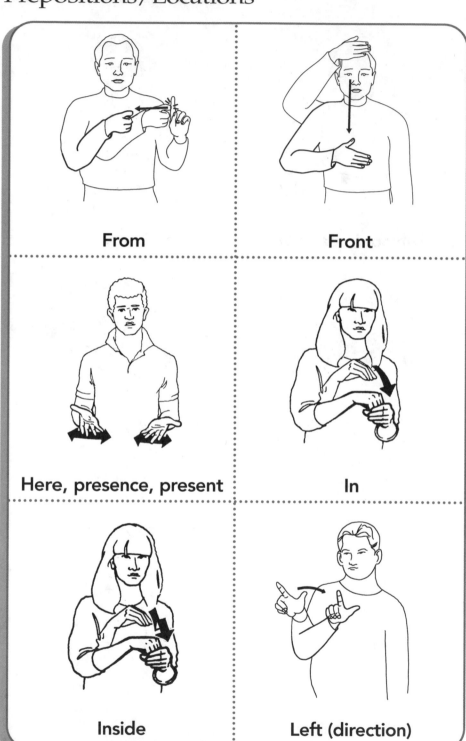

From

Front

Here, presence, present

In

Inside

Left (direction)

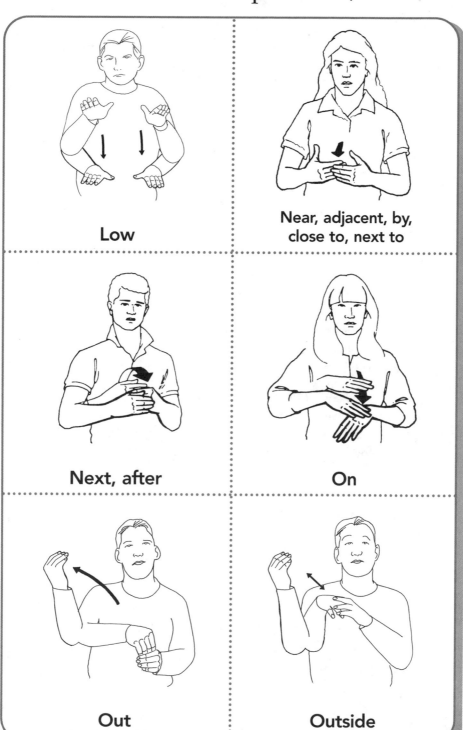

Low

Near, adjacent, by, close to, next to

Next, after

On

Out

Outside

Practice Makes Perfect

Good opportunities for practicing sign language can arise almost anywhere, but here are some of the more obvious places.

School

1. You can practice new signs with your friends over lunch or in the hallways between classes.
2. If there are deaf students in your classes who have interpreters, try watching the interpreters. Keep in mind there may be a few seconds time lag for interpreters to process information, so watch for the signs after you hear the information.
3. Plug your ears and use your eyes instead, but only if your teacher allows you to tape the class. Don't compromise your own education for the sake of learning sign.

Extracurricular Activities

1. Incorporate signs into your club activities (Scouts, 4-H).
2. Use signs for sports skills, coach commands, and plays. The origin of the football huddle is attributed to teams from deaf schools or clubs who were hiding their game plans from rival teams.

Community Activities

1. Community center and religious activities often have interpreters. In fact, many churches and synagogues have translated hymns and prayers into ASL for their deaf congregants.
2. A variety of activities are offered specifically for new signers. Check to see if your area has Silent Dinners.
3. Interpreting and ASL student resources are easily found through internet searches.

Deaf Community Activities

Deaf events abound throughout the country to provide deaf people with access to the richness of everyday living. There are deaf religious groups, deaf sports clubs/teams, deaf social clubs, and deaf political groups, to name a few. Find a group that suits your interests and go join them to expand your signing experience. Deaf theatrical events make for excellent exposure to the richness of ASL.

Don't forget it is as important to learn to understand sign as it is to sign yourself—if you are not sure what other signers are saying, stop them and ask for clarification. They will appreciate your honesty and effort—if not, find someone else to talk with. Deaf people as a whole group are not immune to rudeness and a few of them may be impatient with beginning signers, just as some hearing people may be impatient with people who stutter or deaf people whose speech is difficult to understand.

Prepositions/Locations

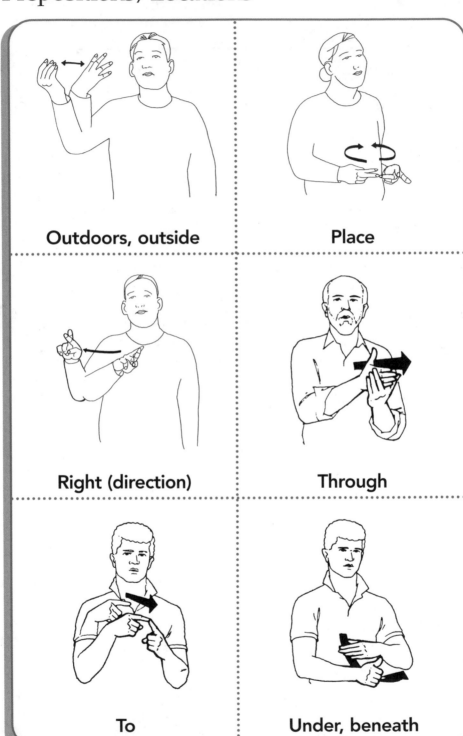

Outdoors, outside

Place

Right (direction)

Through

To

Under, beneath

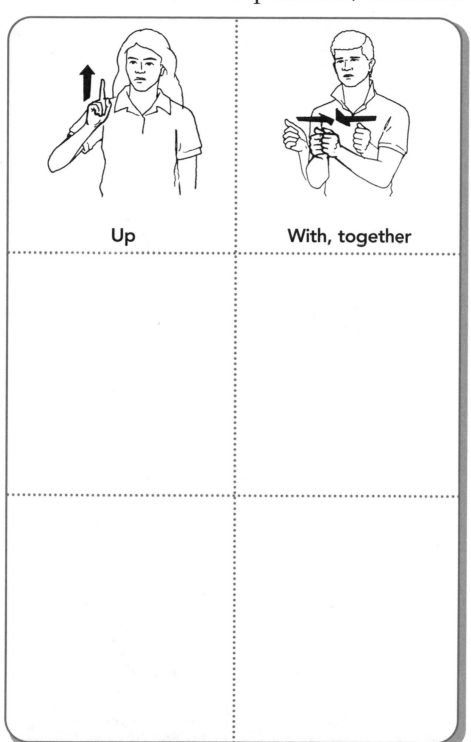

Up

With, together

Quantity

Add to

Add up, accumulate, calculate, sum, total

All, entire

Almost, nearly

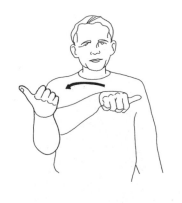

Another

Any

Benefit

Both

Broke

Charge, cost, price

Check (n)

Cost, price

Quantity

Dime

Dollar

Each, every, apiece

Eight

Either

Empty, available, blank, vacant

Enough, adequate, sufficient

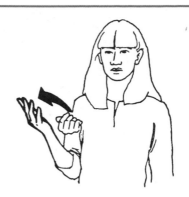

Few, several

First

Five

Four

Full

Quantity

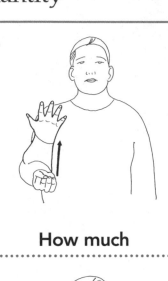

How much

Interest

Last, end, final, lastly

Less

Many, lots, numerous

Maximum

Money, cash, funds

More

Most

Much, a lot

Nine

None

Quantity

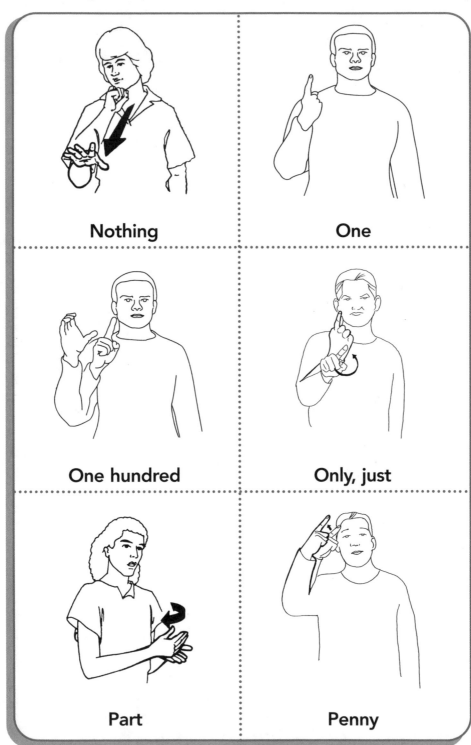

Nothing

One

One hundred

Only, just

Part

Penny

Percent

Quarter

Seven

Six

Some

Something

Quantity

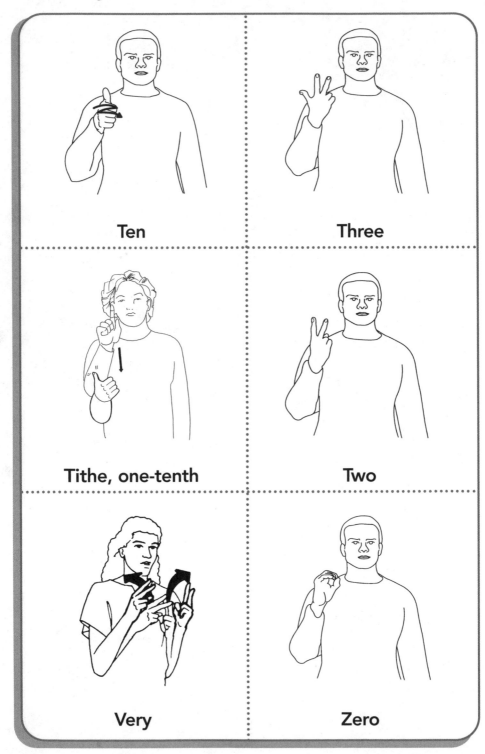

Ten

Three

Tithe, one-tenth

Two

Very

Zero

Ask (a question)

Ask (request)

How

What

When

Where

It's Not Polite to Point—Or is It?

There's a charming little nose twitch known as the "uh-huh" in ASL. One side of the nose wrinkles up—this means the same thing as nodding, but has a slightly more nonchalant feel to it. Try wrinkling up your nose, then try one side only. Not all signers use this, but many from deaf schools are accustomed to this type of facially expressed ASL.

Fluent signers are also very adept at using their eyes and brows, along with head movements, to communicate entire concepts. For example, the following sentence is a request to take note of a subject for private discussion: "Hey, look over there, hmm? Now follow me." In ASL this would be expressed as: *raise eyebrows—direct eye contact with listener—eyes dart in direction of subject—direct eye contact with listener again—slightly lower eyes and nod head in direction of private place to go and talk, eyes flicker there quickly—eye contact once more.* Then the two signers would go talk about the subject in private.

Pointing is a sensitive matter in ASL—it is rude to point outright at someone else if you plan to turn your back to that person and confer in private. No deaf person would ever miss the inference and you would be greatly resented for it. Other than that, pointing functions nicely as a reference in place of nouns or pronouns, and of course, it establishes the subject firmly. POINT, JOHN, HIS SISTER = "That's John's sister" is one example of appropriate pointing.

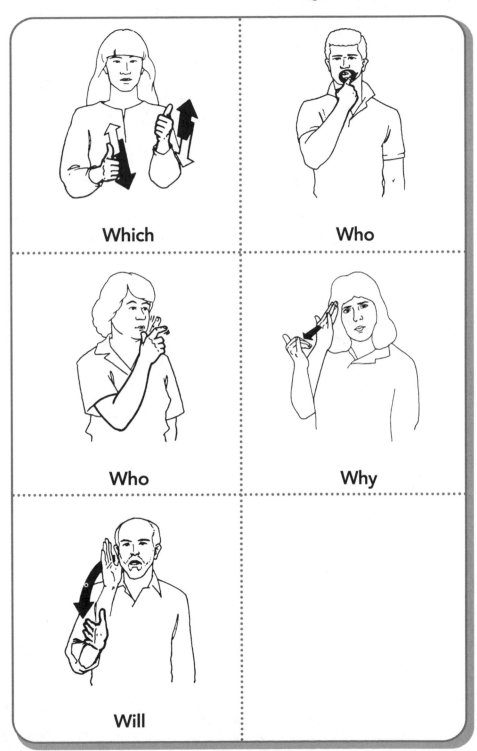

Which

Who

Who

Why

Will

Thoughts/Emotions

Afraid, frighten, frightened, scare, scared, terrified, terrify

Agree, all-in-favor, deal

Angry, furious, mad

Believe

Boiling mad

Bored

Cry, weep

Cry, sob

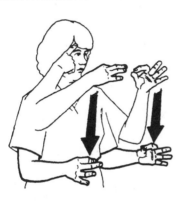

Decide, decision

Disappointed

Discontented, unsatisfied

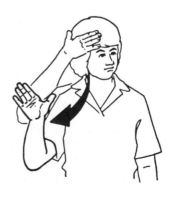

Don't know

Thoughts/Emotions

Don't like

Don't want

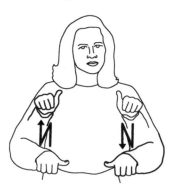

Doubt, unsure

Doubt, don't believe, disbelieve, skeptical

Dream

Embarrassed

Emotion

Enjoy

**Enjoy, appreciate,
enjoyable**

Fall-in-love

Feel, feelings, sense

Fine

Making Faces

In addition to the main components of signs—handshape, location, movement, and palm orientation—facial expression is very important. The face carries the tone or mood throughout the conversation, similar to how voice inflection informs the listener if the speaker is stressed or relaxed.

Facial expression can range from dignified composure to exuberance, from worried to joyful. However, the importance of the facial component is not limited just to mood—there are certain facial expressions, especially mouth movements, that must accompany particular signs. For instance, you should not open your mouth wide when signing LITTLE or SMALL; likewise, you should not purse your lips into a tiny O when signing ENORMOUS.

The idea that sign language can be learned entirely with the hands is adequate when you first begin to study ASL, but once you are comfortable conversing in sign language, you will notice how your whole face and body work along with your hands. Perhaps this is why ASL is considered a language in which it is difficult to lie—fluent signers are able to read another signer's body language and discern when stress is present. Expressing emotion is an individual thing, and each of us controls how much we divulge, but deaf people are quick to notice when someone is tired, upset, or holding something back. Just think, deaf people might not shout with their voices, but with the speed and intensity of their signs and facial expressions, they certainly can "yell." And they can tell when someone is "yelling" at them.

Frustration

Habit, accustom, custom

Happy, cheerful, gay, glad, merry

Hate, abhor, despise, detest, loathe

Idea

Know

Thoughts/Emotions

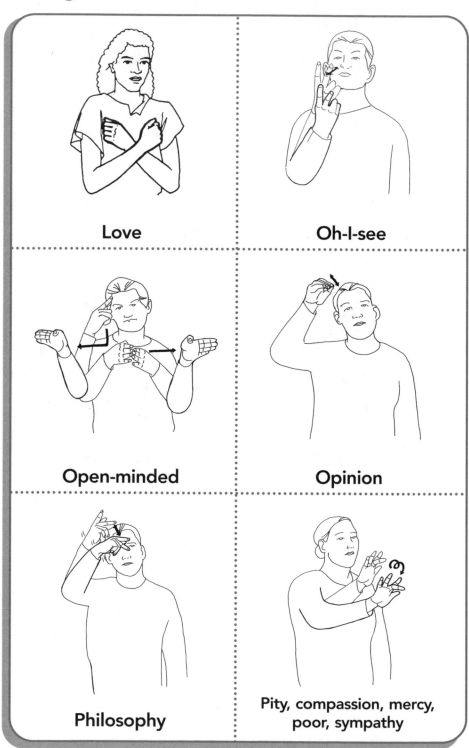

Love

Oh-I-see

Open-minded

Opinion

Philosophy

Pity, compassion, mercy, poor, sympathy

Prefer, preference, rather

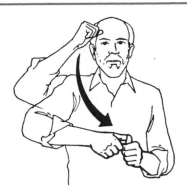

Remember, recall, recollect

Seem, apparent, apparently, appear

Sensitive

Sorry, apologize, apology, pardon, regret

Suppose, if

Thoughts/Emotions

Suspect, suspicious

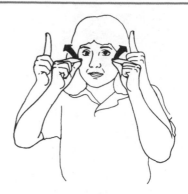

Surprise, surprised, amazed, astonished

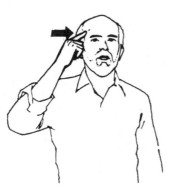

Think, sense

Understand, comprehend, oh-I-see, see

Vanity, vain

Want

Wish, desire

Wonder, ponder, think over

Worry, trouble

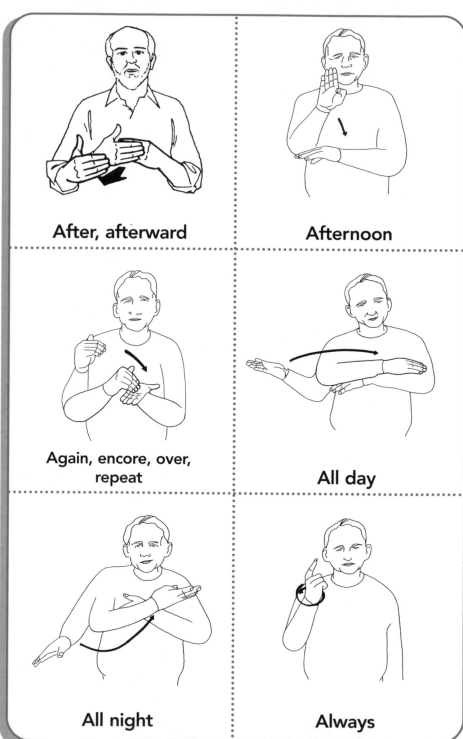

After, afterward

Afternoon

Again, encore, over, repeat

All day

All night

Always

Before, ago, a while ago,
back, ever, last, past,
previous, previously

Before (time)

Clock

Cold, chilly, frigid, winter

Cool, pleasant

Daily, everyday

Dark, shade

Day

During, over, while

Early

Evening

Fall, autumn

Friday

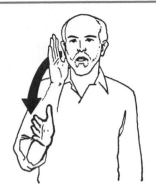

Future

Hour

Late, tardy, yet

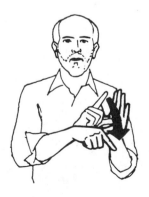

Later, after a while

Later, in a while

Time

In ASL, verb signs don't change to show tense the way English verbs change. Instead, signers use a time sign at the beginning of the sentence to indicate when the action occurred. For the present, the signer will sign NOW or TODAY; to show that something will happen in the future, the signer begins with FUTURE or TOMORROW; and to indicate the past, the signer can start with a specific time indicator, like YESTERDAY or RECENTLY, or a general indicator, like BEFORE, LONG-AGO, or FINISH. Then, the signer uses the basic form of the verb, no matter what tense has been indicated.

To show the progressive tense *(running, jumping, looking)* the signer repeats the verb sign several times. This way, the signer conveys the message that the action continued for a while. Signers also vary the size and movement of their signs depending on how long an action continued. For example, to explain that an action occurs regularly, a signer uses small, quick movements. To show that an action took place over a long period of time, the signer uses large, circular movements.

Now   **Future**   **Before**

Time/Days of the Week/Seasons/Weather

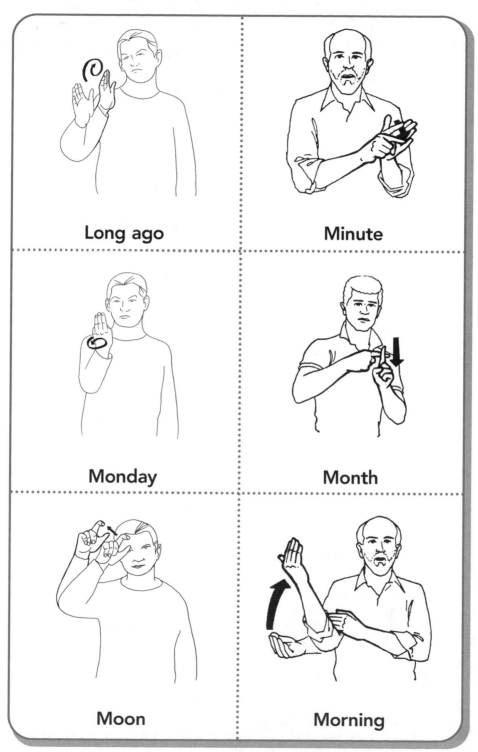

Long ago

Minute

Monday

Month

Moon

Morning

Nature, natural, naturally, normal, of course

Never

Night

Noon

Now, present

Often, frequent, frequently

Rain

Recently, a short time ago, just

Same-time, simultaneously

Saturday

Snow

Soon, brief, shortly

Spring

Sprinkle

Summer

Sun

Sunday

Then

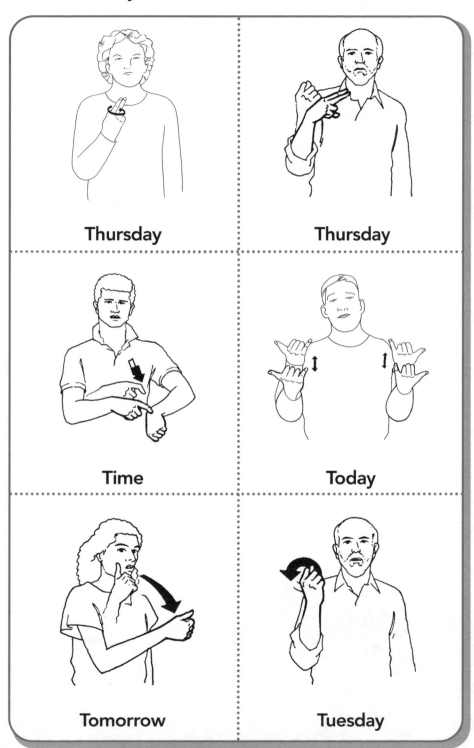

Thursday

Thursday

Time

Today

Tomorrow

Tuesday

Weather	**Wednesday**
Week	**Weekend**
Wind	**Year**

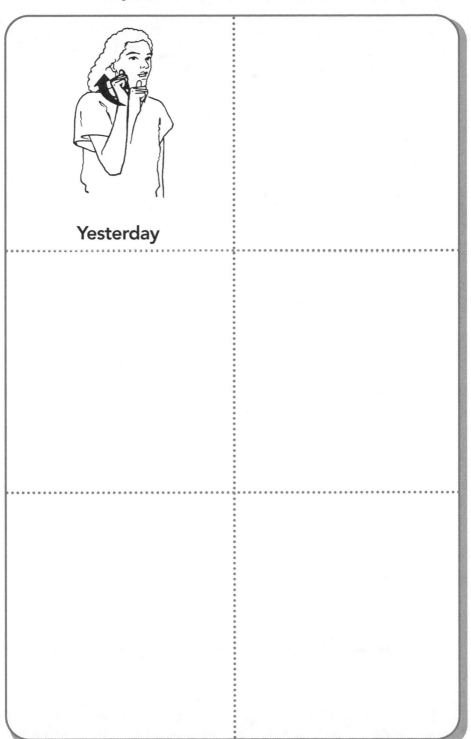

Yesterday

Transportation/Travel

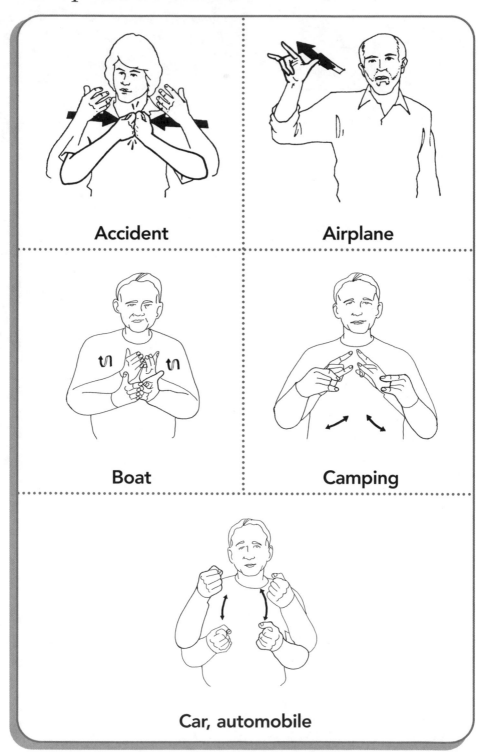

Accident

Airplane

Boat

Camping

Car, automobile

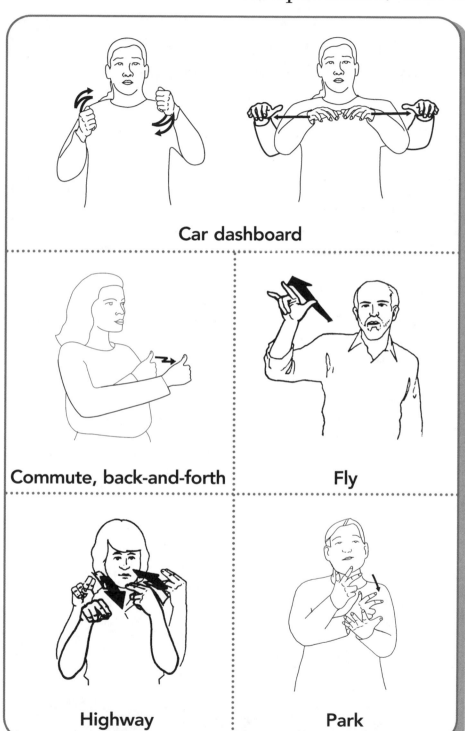

Car dashboard

Commute, back-and-forth

Fly

Highway

Park

Cultural Quirks Among Signers

When meeting new people, fluent signers usually fingerspell their names, and, sometimes, show their name signs as well. At subsequent encounters, names aren't commonly used in greetings. Names do come up in conversation and are used when one person asks another person to get a third party's attention. The exception to this cultural tendency occurs when someone blurts out an admonishment ("Selina! Why did you do that?") or wants to add extra emphasis, perhaps in a teasing mood, ("Joshua...").

In a roomful of signers, especially when they're deaf, someone who leaves the room will inform others where she is going—even if it's just to the bathroom. No one quite seems to know why this happens, but one explanation may be "out of sight, out of mind." Since deaf people can't hear what's happening in the next room, announcing a departure lets everyone else know that the person is not disappearing for the rest of the evening, only for a few minutes. This is one way deaf people stay connected to each other beyond the immediate walls.

When two signers are conversing and walking at the same time, it is common practice and good manners for them to be alert for obstacles in each other's paths. The person who notices an obstacle, like an orange cone or a pole or another passerby, will make sure his or her companion moves around the barrier. This process is practically automatic in native signers and is usually accompanied with a quick wave of the hand or by pulling on the other signer's elbow. Visual scanning while carrying on a converstion may be awkward at first for new signers, but it is not so different from seeing something out of the corner of your eye when you are driving.

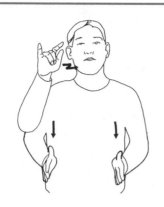

Pilot

Ticket

Train

Travel, journey, tour, trip

Vacation, holiday, leave

Visit

Verbs/Action Words

Accept, adopt

Allow, let

Announce, announcement, declare, proclaim

Appear, show up

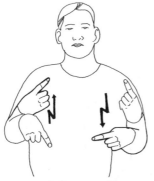

Argue, debate, dispute, quarrel

Arrive

Associate, each other, interact, mingle, socialize

Assume, estimate, guess

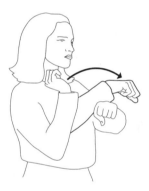

Beat, conquer, defeat, overcome

Be careful, take care of, watch out

Begin, commence, originate, start

Blame, charge

Verbs/Action Words

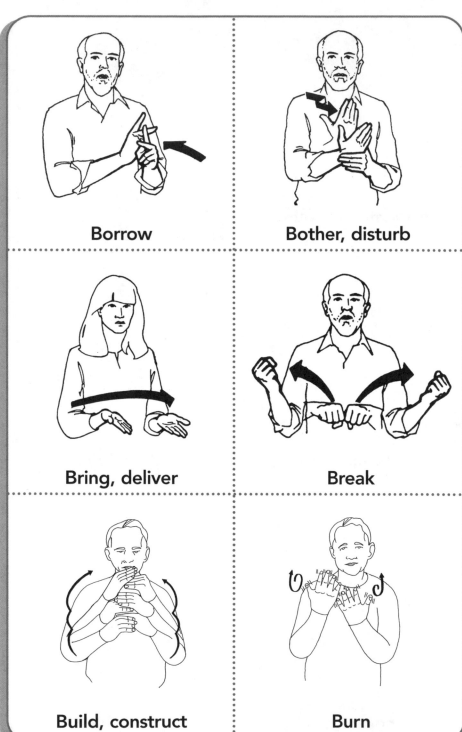

Borrow

Bother, disturb

Bring, deliver

Break

Build, construct

Burn

Buy, purchase

Can, able, could

Cancel, call off

Can't, couldn't, unable

Carry

Catch

Verbs/Action Words

Cause

Change, adapt, adjust, alter, modify, turn into

Chase

Choose, pick, select

Clap, applaud, commend

Clean-up

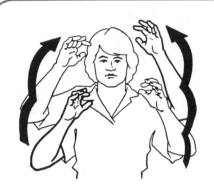

Climb

Close, shut

Collapse, breakdown

Collect, accumulate, gather, reap

Comb hair

Come

Verbs / Action Words

Compare, comparison

Compete, competition, contest

Complain, object

Confront, approach, encounter, face, face-to-face

Connect, attach, belong, join, relate to, unite

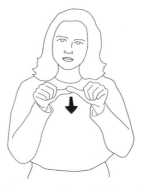

Continue, endure, last, lasting, move on, permanent

Give and Take

Most verbs are signed along with the subject and object of the sentence. These are called *regular* verbs, and they rarely change in movement or location. The movement of some regular verbs reflects the meaning of the sign. For example, for DONATE, the hands move out from the body, to show the signer is giving away something; for TAKE, the hand moves in toward the body, to show the signer has grabbed something to bring with him.

Some verbs can use space to incorporate both the subject and object of the sentence in the verb sign itself. These *directional* verbs use movement to or from the signer to express who or what gives or receives the action. Examples of directional verbs are GIVE, HELP, INFORM, DEFEND, and BORROW/LOAN. Directional verbs are very efficient since an entire sentence is expressed with the use of one sign. To sign I-GIVE-YOU, the signer's hands move toward the person receiving whatever is being given. To sign YOU-GIVE-ME, the signer's hands start away from the body and then move in. With some directional verbs, the palm orientation, not the movement, changes. For example, in the sign POOR-ME, the palm faces in toward the body, but for POOR-YOU the palm faces out.

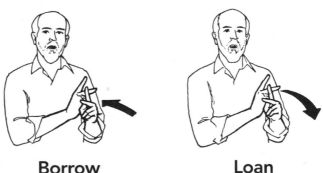

Borrow   **Loan**

Locational verbs are signed on or near the area of the body to which the action refers. Signing HURT near the mouth indicates a toothache; near the head, a headache; and so on. Similarly, signing SURGERY near the appendix versus signing it near the heart gives clear information about what kind of surgery was performed.

Verbs/Action Words

Control, command, direct, govern, manage, regulate, reign, rule, run

Convince

Copy, duplicate, imitate, parrot

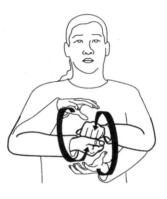

Crush

Cut

Cut off, end

Dance

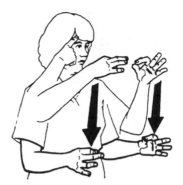

Decide, decision, determine

Delete, eliminate, remove

Demonstration, example, reveal, sample, show

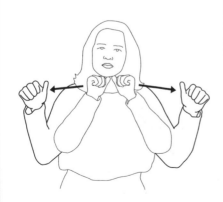

Deny

Depend, count on, rely on

Verbs/Action Words

Deposit

Deteriorate

Disappear, vanish

Disappoint, miss

Discuss

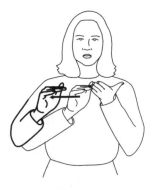

Dismiss, discharge, excuse, exempt, waive

Disturb, annoy, bother

Do, act

Do work

Draw, illustrate

Drive

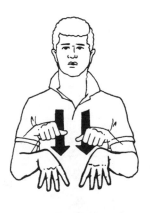

Drop

Verbs/Action Words

Earn, make

Emphasize, impress, stress

Exercise

Expand

Explain, define, describe

Fall

Find, discover, locate

Follow

Fool, trick

Forget

Gain weight

Gardening

Verbs/Action Words

Get, acquire, obtain, receive

Give, contribute

Give up, surrender

Go, attend

Grow, raise

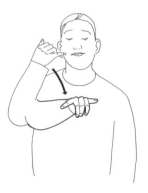

Hang up phone

Verbs / Action Words

Have, own, possess

Hire, invite, welcome

Hold

Hurry, rush

Include, involve, participate

Inform-all, disseminate, notify

Verbs/Action Words

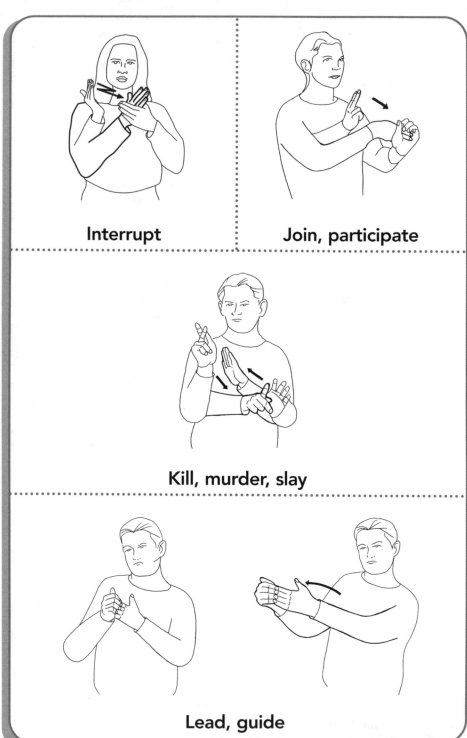

Interrupt

Join, participate

Kill, murder, slay

Lead, guide

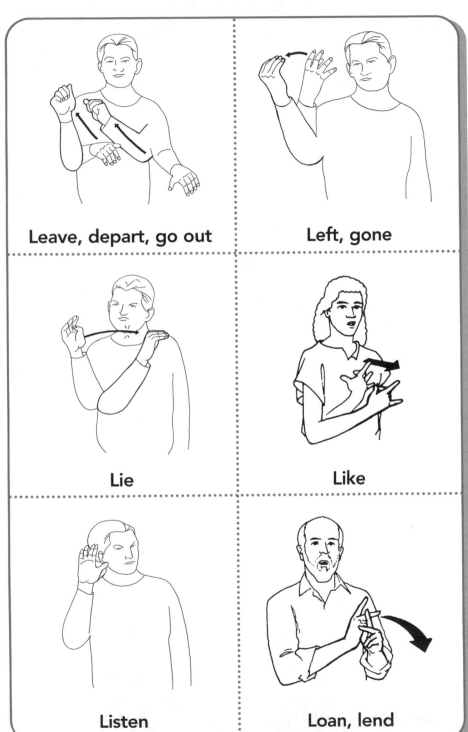

Leave, depart, go out

Left, gone

Lie

Like

Listen

Loan, lend

Verbs/Action Words

Lock

Look, look at

Look-for, explore, search

Lose, lost

Lose (competition)

Make, create, form, produce

Meet

Miss, fail

Misunderstand, miscommunication, misconceive

Move

Need, have to, must, ought, should, supposed to

Related Nouns and Verbs

Signs for related nouns and verbs are formed in very similar ways. In a two-dimensional illustration, the signs may actually look identical because the difference in movements cannot be shown easily. Typically the verb forms have a single large movement, and their noun counterparts are signed smaller and with a double movement Some examples of ASL noun/verb pairs are AIRPLANE and FLY, CHAIR and SIT, and FOOD and EAT.

Airplane

Fly

Another distinction between nouns and verbs is created by adding the *agent marker* to the verb sign. This marker, also known as the *-er* sign or person marker, changes a verb to a noun (for example, TEACH + agent marker = TEACHER). The agent marker also conveys the same idea as the inflections *-an, -ist, -ent,* and *-or* in English (for example, LEARN + agent marker = STUDENT; POLITICS + agent marker = POLITICIAN).

Student

Teacher

Offer, move, present, propose, suggest

Open

Open-window

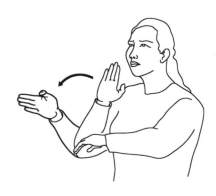

Over-do, cross-wide

Overflow

Owe, afford, debt, due

Verbs/Action Words

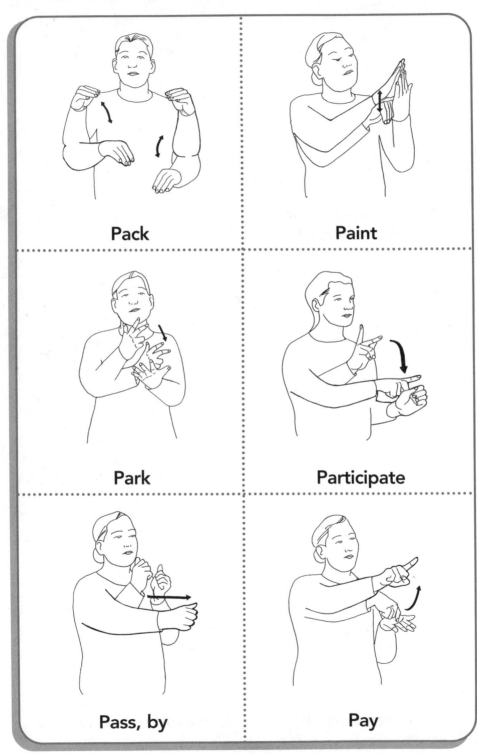

Pack

Paint

Park

Participate

Pass, by

Pay

Persuade

Plan, arrange, order, organize, prepare

Plant

Play, recess

Play-cards, deal

Postpone, delay, put off

Verbs / Action Words

Practice, exercise, rehearse

Praise

Promote, advance, raise

Prove, verify

Pull

Punish, penalize, reprimand

Push, shove

Put

Put-in

Put-in-gas

Put-on-ring

Quit, drop out, withdraw

Verbs / Action Words

Race, compete, competition

Rake

Read

Refuse

Register, sign

Reject, dismiss, exclude

Reject, push away

Remind

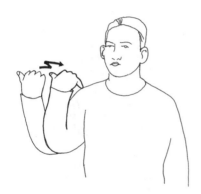

Remind-me

Remove, deduct, delete, discard

Rescue, free, save

Rest

Verbs/Action Words

Retire

Rub, scrub

Ruin, spoil

Run, jog

Run fast

Run (machine)

Run-out-of, all gone,
expire

Satisfy

Save, store

Save, keep, preserve

Say

Scatter, disseminate,
distribute, spread

Verbs/Action Words

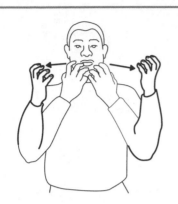

Scream, yell

Seal, certify, stamp

Sell

Send

Send (e-mail, mail)

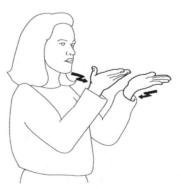

Serve, minister, service, wait on

Sew

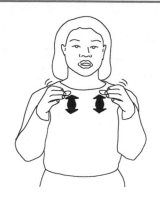

Shake

Show, demonstrate

Sign (language)

Sing, music, song

Smoke

Verbs/Action Words

Solve, dissolve, evaporate, melt, resolve, solution

Spin

Spit

Stand

Stay, remain

Steal, rob

Supervise

Take, grab

Talk, speak

Tell

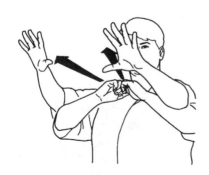

Throw-basketball

Throw-frisbee

Verbs/Action Words

Throw-into-trash

Try, attempt, make an effort

Use, utilize, wear

Use, wear

Wake up

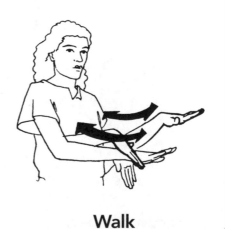

Walk

Wash

Wash-face

Watch, look forward to, observe

Win

Write

Verbs/Action Words

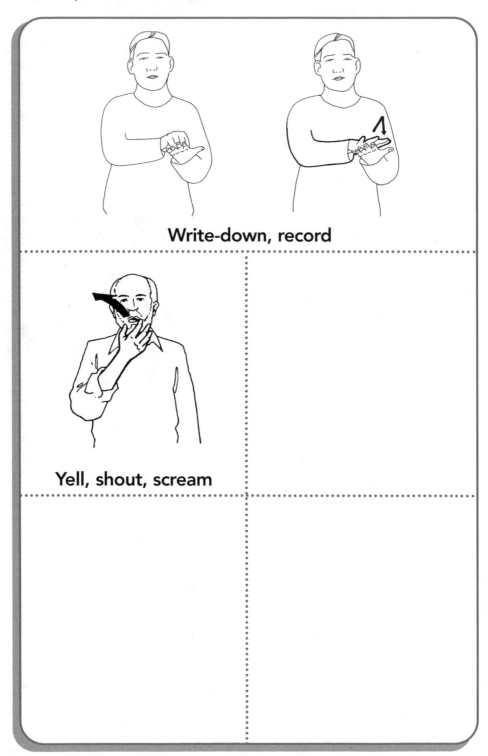

Write-down, record

Yell, shout, scream

Index

To distinguish the same word when used as either a noun or verb, (n) or (v) follows the term. Alphabetization is letter-by-letter (e.g., "addition" precedes "add up").

Index

Index

Index

Index

Index

Index